Whispered Secrets in the

Man Cave:

50 Life Lessons

By RL Collins

Indigo Stone, Publisher

Whispered Secrets in the Man Cave: 50 Life Lessons

Table of Contents

PERSONAL

Beating Your Chest
Hombre. Homme. Rén

What does it mean to be a man in 2021 and beyond? Do not look to the movies, magazines, and celebrities. It is something more organic. And in a lot of ways, it is gender neutral. The world is rolling through major change and transition with the pandemic, political unrest, civil disruption. We need men, women, people who are honest with tact and empathetic.

Honesty with Tact

The world will tell you to be honest. But mostly, people only want to hear a truth they can agree with. If you tell an unpopular truth, you better buckle up! There is going to be hell to pay. It is critical to learn how to tell the truth with a tactfulness. Assume everybody is a delicate soul and easily wounded. But at times, you simply must tell the truth to have progress with challenges and obstacles.

Hard truth: I hate watching that TV show with you, it is so boring!

Tactful Truth: I like spending time with you, maybe we can find a TV show that interests us both.

Hard Truth: This new recipe you used for dinner is unappetizing and falls short of the restaurant version.

Tactful Truth: You used great creativity with tonight's meal, but sometimes less is more.

Using Empathy

In many situations when someone expresses anger, frustration, or difficult emotions in personal relationships – they do not feel seen and heard. Take a moment before you respond. The first impulse might be to dish it right back or lash out with impatience. You just want to bounce to something more pleasant. But wait. Read between the lines. Is this the first time your person has been angry around this topic? Does the situation seem small to you, but real big to them? Are you simply confused and at a lost? Ask questions. Ask a lot of questions. The best resolutions start with, “Help me understand why…” Do not revert to being a helpless victim or barking dog. Ask questions until you understand. Resolve the issue. Squash it. Do not let it fester until there is a total break in communication.

NEXT STEPS: The next time you see or hear something disagreeable with from a loved one, offer a kind redirection instead of a hard complaint.

The world will tell you to be honest. But mostly, people only want to hear a truth they can agree with.

The Good Fight

"Appear weak when you are strong, and strong when you are weak."

— Sun Tzu, The Art of War

We have all had the experience of dealing with someone who brings us unnecessary conflict. You might have to deal with a difficult personality at work, in the neighborhood, or while in line at the local convenience store. It is important to know that most misguided hostility stems from jealousy. Beware the green-eyed monster! The other person perceives you has having more than them in some way or succeeding where they fail.

Appearing Weak When You Are Strong

When dealing with an unstoppable difficult person, there is nothing wrong with presenting yourself as meek so long as you do not *believe* that you are meek. Maintain healthy boundaries. Have a quiet confidence. Soften your voice. The jealous person will calm down, have a little more peace in their life, and not spend so much of their free time plotting your downfall. Jealous people often have a personal story we know nothing about that makes them lash out over unknown issues.

Appearing Strong When You are Weak

Sometimes the sharks are circling, and you must be very, very careful not to leave any blood in the water. The difficult person is always watching you, testing you, poking you. He is waiting for a moment of weakness to say – I gotcha! Like *Marvel's* Iron Man there are situations where you put on your suit of armor and don a mask. Do it! Rock it! Watch your level of vulnerability around people and situations that are consistently negative. More than likely the jealous person you are dealing with is also wearing a mask. She is not willing to voice the real issue so there is this never-ending battle of wills.

Save yourself the drama. Look out for your own best interest. Be Iron Man when you feel like little Bo Peep.

NEXT STEPS: Before entering a difficult meeting, look at yourself in the mirror and say 20 times: "I am a Rockstar!"

It is important to know that most misguided hostility stems from jealousy. Beware the green-eyed monster!

The Exploding Volcano and Mindfulness

Did she just roll her eyes at me?! Did he just slip into my parking spot?! Is this hair in my sandwich?!

The world can test us. Small things turn into big things. We want to beat our chest. We want to spill over like an exploding volcano. Somebody *owes* me!

Sorry sir, but this is not the way. The world is spinning from a pandemic, civil unrest, and political disagreements. We do not need more random anger.

Sometimes, we are short tempered because we are only tired, hungry, or low testosterone. However, family, friends, and co-workers do not understand this if we do not understand it ourselves. Mindfulness is the key to living in an unpredictable world and not becoming part of the problem.

What is Mindfulness?

Mindfulness is a type of meditation where you focus on being keenly aware of what you are sensing and feeling in the moment. You drop the need to interpret or have personal judgment. There are different ways to practice mindfulness. It involves breathing methods, guided imagery, and other practices to relax the body and mind and help reduce stress.

How to Gain Mindfulness?

There are different tips and strategies to mindfulness. Try these:

- Meditate. Taking even just 5 minutes to sit quietly and follow your breath can help you feel more conscious and connected for the rest of your day.
- Focus on one thing at a time
- Slow down
- Eat mindfully. Savor the flavor and texture of each bite of food.
- Limit time on the phone and computer. Set aside time to unplug.

- Move and get some exercise.
- Spend time in nature, get some fresh air, appreciate animals and/or plants

The Benefits of Mindfulness

Mindfulness can help relieve stress, treat heart disease, lower blood pressure, reduce chronic pain, improve sleep, and alleviate gastrointestinal difficulties. You are less likely be an exploding volcano with family, friends, or co-workers. You can navigate your own difficult emotions and be a resource to others.

NEXT STEPS: If you are a beginner, try a guided mediation app or sit in silence and count your breaths for 5 minutes.

Mindfulness is the key to living in an unpredictable world and not becoming part of the problem.

Myth Busting the Macho Man
self-identity

The recognition of one's potential and qualities as an individual, especially in relation to social context.

To know who you are in this world and have unshakeable confidence is a goal worth striving for, yet difficult to obtain. It does not happen overnight. You take it day by day and navigate around constant messaging around what it means to be a man in 2021 and beyond.

The first step is to separate what you want from what other people want. Find your inner voice in the middle of celebrity opinions, political stances, and artificial social constructs.

Values

When defining your values, it helps to have a conversation with yourself. Explore ways to understand who you are. What thoughts and ideas make you feel happy and light? What thoughts and ideas make you feel heavy and apprehensive? We cannot be everything to everybody. Do more of what feels right. Do less of what feels wrong. When a situation occurs, take a step back and process, thoughts, and feelings, without trying to react immediately. Then decide, what is healthy for you, and take that path.

Beliefs

You are who you say you are. If you say you are amazing, you are amazing. If you say you are failing, you are failing. When faced with different situations in life, see them as opportunities to decide who you are and what you stand for. Act in ways that align with your values. How you choose to act, think, and feel are all expressions of who you are. Each day is an opportunity to express the best side of yourself.

Choices

There are a few ways to blend your values and beliefs into your choices for daily life:

- Make decisions that line up with your feelings and logical brain by looking at the facts of every situation.
- Practice sitting with the discomfort. We do not always get what we want when we want it.
- Think about your personal values without imposing them on others or making demands of others.
- Stand strong with your own ideas, values, and thoughts when others disagree with them.
- Act in ways that fit with who you are and bring harmony into your life.

NEXT STEPS: Understand that this post was about you defining who you are as a man, instead of having someone else dictate the definition of manhood.

To know who you are in this world and have unshakeable confidence is a goal worth striving for, yet difficult to obtain.

Real Men Cry

"It's okay to cry, the sky does it too." – Author Unknown

Real men cry. In reality, no sane person will hold it against you. We all know the average man does not cry every day. So, when you reach that point, and you just cannot hold it in any longer, cry. Do not apologize. Do not be embarrassed. Do not over explain.

The world needs more authentic men.

NEXT STEPS: Share this with a father, brother, or nephew.

"It's okay to cry, the sky does it too." – Author Unknown

Kicking Butt with Oral

Sometimes, as a man, you just have step up, be the hero, and slay those dragons! Great men, leaders, friends, and lovers know how to master oral…communication. Words are power!

Considering the pandemic, today's common communication channels often fall to social media. We have tons of tweeting, texting, emailing, and sending lines of code in emojis. However, real human connection, real adult relationships are based on strong, effective communication beyond emojis.

Listen, listen, and listen. People want to know that they are being heard. Really listen to what the other person is saying, instead of organizing your response. Ask questions. Avoid misunderstandings by asking good questions. When you are speaking to someone on the phone, do not respond to an email, or send a text at the same time. The other person will know that she does not have your attention.

Adjust to your audience. It is okay to use acronyms and slang language when you are communicating with a good friend, but if you are emailing or texting your boss, "Hey," "TTYL" or any slang language, has no place in your message. Effective communicators adapt their message based on who they are speaking to, so try to keep the other person in mind, when you are delivering a message.

Body language matters. This is important for face-to-face meetings and video conferencing. Make sure that you appear accessible and have open body language. Do not cross your arms. Keep eye contact so that the other person knows that you are paying attention.

Sometimes you need to pick up the phone. If you find that you have a lot to say, instead of sending an email, call the person instead. Email is great, but sometimes it is easier to communicate what you have to say verbally. And sometimes, just sometimes, hearing a man's voice is super sexy.

Think before you speak. Do not allow difficult emotions or impulsive thoughts to interfere with good communication. Pause before you speak. Do not say the first thing that comes to mind. Take a moment and pay close attention to what you say and how you say it.

Maintain a positive attitude and smile. Nobody likes a *Debbie Downer.* We all have our good days and bad days. Try not to hold anyone hostage in a difficult conversation because you are having a bad day.

NEXT STEPS: Pick up the phone or jump into a personal video conference and have conversation with a good friend.

People want to know that they are being heard.

Life can pull us in different directions. Family, friends, and co-workers need us! People count on us to problem solve, motivate them through difficult times, or to buy milk from the grocery store. How can you get is all done and balance with a certain amount of grace? *Time management.*

Understand You Are Not Perfect

It is okay, you can admit to yourself that you are not perfect. Did you also know that *nobody* is perfect? Take a moment right now to realize it is okay to make mistakes and be imperfect. As you work to improve your time management skills, understand that some plans will fall through. Instead of feeling defeated, rework your plans, and *try again.*

Plan Each Day

You do not have to be a type A personality to plan your days. Even though there is some unpredictability to life, you can still make plans. There are different ways you can do this to be successful. One suggestion is to take a few minutes every night before bed and put together your agenda for the next day. Then take a step back from your list to decide the who, what, when, where, what, why, and how of any intricate responsibilities you have tomorrow. Leave open spaces for breaks and the unexpected.

Prioritize Your Daily, Weekly, & Monthly Tasks

To boost the effectiveness of your private planning sessions, you should identify the priorities for upcoming days, weeks, and even months. Projecting out towards future tasks will allow you to spread your workload out over time so you are not overwhelmed or stressed out. You will be able to establish a structured routine you can live with.

Use Time Management Tools

One of the best things you can do to manage your time more wisely is by using as many tools as necessary to support your position. There are millions of computer programs and smartphone apps out there waiting to make your life easier with a simple download. Make technology work for you!

Finally, Do Not Multitask

Your family and friends might brag about multitasking and slaying dragons, but it makes you less productive. Multitasking can lower your comprehension level and overall intelligence by more than 11%? Beyond your intelligence level, multitasking also inhibits performance with a 40% drop in productivity. Just don't do it and drop that fantasy that it makes you *Superman.*

NEXT STEPS: Open a writing app on your phone and jot down 5 important tasks you have for the week then plan how to get them done.

It is okay, you can admit to yourself that you are not perfect. Did you also know that *nobody* is perfect?

Finances and Self-Esteem Part 1

Let us keep it real, we all need money to provide food, shelter, and clothing for ourselves and our families. Having enough money frees our mind to focus on more than just mere survival. Being well-paid for our talents and abilities is a source of great pride. However, money does not make the man. Money does not make you better or worse than the person next to you in life.

There are different ways to have a healthy self-esteem separate from your financial status in life.

Be mindful

Simply becoming aware of our negative self-talk. Distance yourself from the feelings it brings up. This will help you identify with them less. Without this awareness, we can easily fall into the trap of believing our self-limiting talk. Thoughts are just thoughts; they are not necessarily the facts. Stay in the present. Try mindful eating, savoring the smell, taste, and texture of a meal. Try mindful walking, go outside, and choose a path. Walk and appreciate the feeling of the grass or pavement beneath your feet. Enjoy the fresh air, light rain, or light snow depending on where you are. Try a mediation app on your phone and learn or to navigate life through deep breathing.

Change the Story

We all have an ongoing story we tell ourselves about who we are and the life we have lived. Often, this story comes from messages from family, friends, co-workers, and society at large. You can rewrite this story where you are a lovable, valuable, respected human being. Start with affirmations. What do you wish you believed about yourself? Repeat these phrases to yourself every day.

Do Not Compare Yourself to Others

Comparing yourself to the people around you is a great way to fall down an endless rabbit hole of despair. You must, must accept yourself just the way you are—flaws and all. Just because the person next to you appears happy, it does not mean they are happy.

Comparisons only lead to negative self-talk, which leads to anxiety and stress. Drop it. Be exactly who you are today.

Get Moving

Exercise organizes your day around self-care. If you need to drop a task from your endless to-do list for the sole purpose of relaxation or doing something fun and seeing how that feels. Other forms of self-care, such as proper nutrition and sufficient sleep, have also been shown to have positive effects on one's self-perception.

NEXT STEPS: Read part 2 of "Finances and Self-Esteem." Find a favorite quote from family, friends, or a fun celebrity and put it on a Post-it on your mirror.

There are different ways to have a healthy self-esteem separate from your financial status in life.

Finances and Self-Esteem Part 2

When you define who you are by finances and material things, you are on a rocky road. Money may come and go based on situations outside our control. Pandemics hit and may close a business. Corruption can crash a stock or make an investment run dry. Maybe we have a health crisis and cannot work for a period of time. Anything can happen. To survive in this world, you need a healthy love of self.

There are countless ways to build a healthy self-esteem. Here are more tips to motivate you:

Do unto Others

Treat people the way you want to be treated. Even if the person is being nasty and mean to you, you do not know the story behind it. Be respectful. Be compassionate. Take a step back if you need to. If you want forgiveness and understanding on your dark days, give it to others.

Forgive Yourself and Others

Holding on to feelings of bitterness or resentment, keep us stuck in a cycle of negativity. Is there is someone in your life you have not forgiven? An ex-partner? A family member? Yourself? Forgiveness starts with you. If we have not forgiven yourself, shame will keep you in a loop of negativity. Forgiveness boosts your self-esteem because it connects you with you loving nature and promotes an acceptance of self and others, despite our flaws.

You Are Not Your Circumstances

Money and your financial worth are not static. It can change year to year. It can go up; it can go down. Learn to differentiate between your circumstances and who you are is key to self-worth. Inner worth, loving your imperfect self, providing a strong foundation for personal growth, is *PRICELESS.*

We are all born with infinite potential and equal worth as human beings. That we are anything less is a false belief that we have learned over time. Therefore, with hard work and self-compassion, self-destructive thoughts and beliefs can be unlearned. Start taking steps today to build yourself self-esteem so you can face the world no matter your temporary circumstances.

NEXT STEPS: Stand in the mirror and say: I love me. I like me. I respect me. I am more than enough.

To survive in this world, you need a healthy love of self.

Mastering Negative Self-Talk

Life, real life is a series of successes and failures. Sometimes we feel as if we are on top of the mountain. And sometimes, we feel low in the valley. How we talk to ourselves when we are low in the valley, determines how quickly we bounce back. No matter the size of your personal circle of family, friends, and co-workers, *YOU* should be the biggest cheerleader in your life. *Always talk to yourself with kindness, compassion, and forgiveness.*

What is Negative Self-Talk?

Negative self-talk is a common battle many of us must face from time to time. Negative self-talk is feeling disappointed that we were not perfect in a certain situation. Negative self-talk is thinking in absolutes and extremes. It is believing in terms around "you always" or "you never." Failure is perceived to be a way of life, instead of a temporary, normal set back that happens to all us from time to time. Negative self-talk can spiral into depression, anxiety, and chronic insomnia if not properly addressed.

How to Beat Negative Self-Talk?

Do not try to stop your thoughts. It is impossible. Acknowledge you have difficult feelings. Try to diagnose why. Replace them with a better alternative.

Are you a planner? If a project failed, figure out how to revise your steps to get better results next time. If a relationship failed, accept your part, and only your part. You have no control over the thoughts and actions of others. What can you learn to do differently with the next companion? If you set a personal goal and fell short, sometimes, just sometimes, it was not meant to be. What is the second-best goal you can obtain?

Are you more spiritual? Words have power. Replace your negative self-talk with affirmations, mantras, poetry of love. You can find free resources online and collect positive affirmations and quotes that you can say each day. Depending on your faith, every religion has spiritual mantras to connect you to a higher Power. Release yourself from trying to control everything in your life. Listen to motivational podcasts or YouTube videos and simply tap into good feelings as needed, whenever you need it.

Do you like to get physical? Practice mindfulness, deep breathing, and exercise. Mindfulness is being in the moment and not focusing on the past or the future. You can practice mindfulness through meditation. You might start with just 5 minutes a day. Practice mindful breathing. Appreciate being alive when others have already crossed over. You do not have to be an athlete to appreciate exercise. You can go for a walk outside. Dance to a YouTube video for 5 minutes. You can do some stretching before going to bed. Keep to simple. Allow small accomplishments to replace your negative self-talk.

NEXT STEPS: Realize that you are not alone. The fact that you are reading this article, means others have the same struggle as you.

No matter the size of your personal circle of family, friends, and co-workers, *YOU* should be the biggest cheerleader in your life.

Having unshakeable confidence is the key to navigating a world of pandemics, political stances, and civil unrest. Healthy self-confidence helps us step out into the unknown and walk our own unique path. Without some level of confidence, we are defeated before we begin.

What is self-confidence? Self-confidence is not the same thing as self-esteem. A healthy self-esteem means you place a high value on yourself. You have strong self-worth. You like yourself. Self-confidence is the belief you can accomplish different goals regardless of your actual skill level.

How do you build self-confidence? Having unshakeable confidence is changing the beliefs you have about yourself and it takes work. Building and maintaining healthy confidence takes daily practice. You do not just *arrive,* then magically you are done for life.

Step 1: Try things outside your comfort zone

Stepping outside your comfort zone is, as you might expect, uncomfortable. Real confidence is the ability to be comfortable in a variety of situations that would make most people uncomfortable. You can challenge yourself in large and small ways. For example, you might take on a new job or confront someone you usually avoid. Maybe you strike up a conversation with someone new if you are normally shy. Maybe you try a new cuisine at a restaurant. It is more important you regularly challenge your comfort zone in small ways rather than jump off the deep end in major ways.

Step 2: Try a new look

How you dress can affect how other people perceive you, but it can also affect how you perceive yourself. Wearing different clothes can prompt you to think or behave differently. This effect is not just limited to feeling good about yourself. For example, if you want that management job, try wearing a tie from time to time. Look the part, even if you have not actually been hired. If you want to feel more confident, dress the way a confident version of yourself would.

Step 3: Use powerful body language

Much like how you dress, your posture and body language can affect how you feel about yourself. This might seem small—try out powerful stances. Great posture can help adjust your frame of mind. When you are closing a deal in business, plant your hands on the table and lean forward. When you are pitching an idea, rest your feet on the table, clasp your hands behind your head, and lean back. Before an interview, plant your feet widely and stretch your arms overhead in a V shape. When talking to your boss, puff out your chest, plant your hands on your hips, and stand with feet hip-width apart.

NEXT STEPS: This article is not an exhaustive list of confidence boosting techniques, they are strategies you can start doing TODAY!

Building and maintaining healthy confidence takes daily practice. You do not just *arrive,* then magically you are done for life.

The Resilient Warrior

"Strength does not come from winning. Your struggles develop your strengths. When you go through hardships and decide not to surrender, that is strength." — Mohandas Gandhi

The most basic definition of resilience is an ability to recover from or adjust easily to misfortune or change. You must imagine yourself to be a rubber band to navigate in this world of pandemics, political stances, and civil unrest. You stretch. You bounce back. No matter what, your strength lies in your ability to recover from stresses and challenges.

There are multiple benefits to becoming a resilient warrior:

- Improved relationships
- Improved coping when we experience emotional disruptions
- Improved working memory
- Improved immune system function and sleep
- Decreased depressive symptoms & increased emotional well-being

There are great and simple ways to build resilience that are approved by the American Psychological Association.

- Make connections. Good relationships with close family members, friends, or others are important.
- Accept help and support from those who care about you and will listen to you strengthens resilience.
- Some people find that being active in civic groups, faith-based organizations, or other local groups provides social support and can help with reclaiming hope. Assist others in their time of need also can benefit the helper.
- Avoid seeing crises as insurmountable problems. You cannot change the fact that highly stressful events happen, but you can change how you interpret and respond to these events.
- Accept that change is a part of living. Certain goals may no longer be attainable because of adverse situations. Accepting

circumstances that cannot be changed can help you focus on circumstances that you can alter.

- Move toward your goals. Develop some realistic goals. Do something regularly -- even if it seems like a small accomplishment -- that enables you to move toward your goals. Instead of focusing on tasks that seem unachievable.
- Take care of yourself. Pay attention to your own needs and feelings. Engage in activities that you enjoy and find relaxing. Exercise regularly.
- Additional ways of strengthening resilience may be helpful. For example, some people write about their deepest thoughts and feelings related to trauma or other stressful events in their life. Meditation and spiritual practices help some people build connections and restore hope.

No matter your circumstances, imagine yourself to be that rubber band. Face challenges head on, be willing to stretch, but do not let it break you. Build a positive support team and be willing to help others.

NEXT STEPS: Reach out to a struggle loved one and tell her, "I am here for you" and mean it.

No matter what, your strength lies in your ability to recover from stresses and challenges.

Redemption

Sometimes life smacks you in the face. You did not even see it coming. Maybe you are blindsided by a job loss. Maybe you are surprised by the passing of a loved one. Maybe you are used to a certain way of doing things, then the rules change. The world can be unpredictable.

After you roll through the anger, grief, and uncertainty – you have a decision to make. Stay stuck or rebuild? Choosing to rebuild your life, heart, or mind is the mark of maturity. You can rebuild stronger and wiser. You may even reach a point where the past is simply a lesson learned.

Writing can help you process difficult situations. Through journaling you can be brutally honest. You can write and write, until there is no more to say. Then you start to plan for a better future. Use the journal to set goals, timeframes, and problem solve. Be your own cheerleader during the reconstruction. Redeem yourself – make a comeback!

Keeping a journal is easy and inexpensive. It never gets tired of listening to you. You can be as silly or angry as you want. You can brainstorm plans and ideas until you are ready to make them reality. Set aside a few minutes each day to write. It is for your eyes only.

NEXT STEPS: Grab a piece of paper or open a writing app on your phone and write whatever comes to mind.

Writing can help you process difficult situations.

Saying "I'm Sorry!"

Sometimes we really screw things up. You are not the victim— you are the one who stirred sh*t up! It is important to know how to give a genuine apology. If you want to repair the relationship, asking for forgiveness is key.

According to relationship experts, *Paired Life*, apologizing to your partner involves more than just saying "I'm sorry." There are many things you can do—from taking responsibility for your actions to resisting the urge to pull out the so-called "scorecard"—that will make your apology come across sincerely.

How to Give a Sincere and Heartfelt Apology

- Avoid using the word "but."
- Do not take your partner's forgiveness for granted. Ask—but do not demand—that you be forgiven for your mistake.
- Do not blame your partner for how you behaved. Take responsibility for the hurtful things that you said and did.
- Express your gratitude for your partner's patience.
- Choose words and phrases that are soft, gentle, and sincere, but make sure they sound like things you would actually say. Do not try to be someone else when you apologize for your blunder. Being fake is the worst way to say sorry!
- If you are writing a note to say sorry to your lover, put some thought into your writing materials. A handwritten card is far more personal and sincere than a message sent by text or email.

An apology is the superglue of life. It can repair just about anything. We all make mistakes. Admitting your mistakes and making repairs are the marks of maturity. Unless you are rich and famous, you do not have endless friends and lovers. Learn to give a heartfelt apology.

NEXT STEPS: Is there someone you need to apologize to today?

Unless you are rich and famous, you do not have endless friends and lovers. Learn to give a heartfelt apology.

What does Mansplaining mean?

Mansplaining is, at its core, a very specific thing. It is what occurs when a man talks condescendingly to someone (especially a woman) about something he has incomplete knowledge of, with the mistaken assumption that he knows more about it than the person he is talking to does.

Bottomline, do not do this please. Thank you!

Update: The word mansplaining was added to Merriam-Webster dictionary in March 2018.

NEXT STEPS: If you do not know a certain topic, just sit there, and look cute.

Avoid mansplaining at all costs!

Having healthy competition in life can keep your mind, body, and soul in tip top shape. Use competitive feelings to help motivate you not destroy others — or yourself. Be respectful, ethical, cooperative, personally accountable, and non-threatening. *Climb the proverbial mountain and plant your flag!*

There are different ways to incorporate a bit of healthy competition in life, beyond the playing field or the boardroom. *Life Zemplified* has some great suggestions:

Healthy Competition with Personal Finances

Challenge some friends to save money or pay off debt. Or use the net worth of others to motivate yourself to earn and save more. Challenge your spouse to some no spend months. Or invite others to evaluate their efforts towards the pursuit of financial independence and early retirement for some healthy comparisons.

Healthy Competition in Fitness

Challenge yourself to improve your 1-mile walking pace. Design a mini-obstacle race in your backyard for the kids. See who can do more jumping jacks in 1 minute, you or your partner. Sign-up for a 5K race with a friend, slowest finisher buys beer.

Healthy Competition with Food

Challenge a coworker or two to brown bag lunch for a month. Have a home "Chopped" game with friends or family. Strive to eat 10 servings of vegetables a day. Challenge your spouse or a friend to a recipe creation contest – let the kids participate.

Healthy Competition, Keep It Fun!

Play, engage with others, and have fun. The things we and others consider fun is an endless list. Just about any hobby can also be made competitive by challenging yourself as well as others. Keep it healthy and fun by respecting other's feelings (and your own), be honest, respectful, and most of all, be able to lose, as well as win. Then challenge yourself to do better next time.

NEXT STEPS: What healthy competition can you schedule for the next weekend?

Having healthy competition in life can keep your mind, body, and soul in tip top shape.

Stronger Together

At times in life, the weight on our shoulders is too much to bear. Know when to ask for help. We are stronger together.

While mental illnesses affect both men and women, the prevalence of mental illnesses in men is often lower than women. Men with mental illnesses are also less likely to have received mental health treatment than women in the past year. However, men are more likely to die by suicide than women, according to the *Centers for Disease Control and Prevention.* Recognizing the signs that you or someone you love may have a mental disorder is the first step toward getting treatment. The earlier that treatment begins, the more effective it can be.

Warning Signs

Men and women can develop most of the same mental disorders and conditions but may experience different symptoms. Some symptoms include:

- Anger, irritability, or aggressiveness
- Noticeable changes in mood, energy level, or appetite
- Difficulty sleeping or sleeping too much
- Difficulty concentrating, feeling restless, or on edge
- Increased worry or feeling stressed
- Misuse of alcohol and/or drugs
- Sadness or hopelessness
- Suicidal thoughts
- Feeling flat or having trouble feeling positive emotions
- Engaging in high-risk activities
- Aches, headaches, digestive problems without a clear cause
- Obsessive thinking or compulsive behavior
- Thoughts or behaviors that interfere with work, family, or social life
- Unusual thinking or behaviors that concern other people

Mental disorders can be treated. If you are unsure where to go for help, ask your family doctor or visit NIMH's Help for Mental Illnesses webpage. Communicating well with your health care provider can improve your care and help you both make good choices about your health. Read about tips to help prepare and get the most out of your visit. For additional resources, including questions to ask your health care provider, visit the Agency for Healthcare Research and Quality.

Source: National Institute of Mental Health, Men and Mental Health

NEXT STEPS: If you or someone you know is in a crisis, get help immediately. You can call 911 or the National Suicide Prevention Line at 1-800-273-TALK (8255).

Mental disorders can be treated.

Calm and clear your mind. Consider your struggles and successes. When you wake up in the morning do you choose to try again? Or just lay in bed defeated? If you choose to try again, that is the silver lining. Write it down. Hold on to it.

Keeping a journal can help you commit to seeing the positive side of life and set goals. Your ideas to overcome challenges may be fuzzy at first. However, the process of writing and rewriting can create a laser focus.

Try to set aside fifteen to twenty minutes a day to journal. Review your goals, think about your options to accomplish tasks, then prioritize. If possible, write around the same time each day.

Journaling allows you to record progress. If you have struggles or setbacks you can record it in your journal. Then you work through to solutions and see the silver lining. If you ever have a difficult day, you can take out your journal and review the progress you have made.

Writing is an opportunity to explore your feelings and address barriers to your progress. Sometimes we are our own worst enemy. We do not believe in ourselves. We let doubts hold us back. We have negative self-talk. Journal all the negative feelings. Release them. Then plan realistic next steps to achieving your important goals.

Finally, journaling can help you keep the ball rolling. Vent the difficult emotions. Identify the silver lining. Create a to do list. Each day before you close the journal, give yourself an assignment. Choose something you can accomplish in the next 24-48 hours.

NEXT STEPS: Pick a journal for yourself. It can be as plain or as fancy as you want. Start writing!

Keeping a journal can help you commit to seeing the positive side of life and set goals.

Grit vs. IQ

I think I can. I think I can. Grit.

To be successful in this world, you need more than just IQ points. Grit, the ability to persevere, will carry you through the darkest times.

Grit is not really taught in schools today. If you struggle in school, you get a low grade, then you move on to the next lessons. You may or may not get the chance to improve. You may or may not even understand *how* you missed the mark.

Real grit and determination mean you take a hard look at what is not working, diagnose the problem, then take steps to correct it. The correction may happen in a few minutes, few days, or few months. But you keep at it until you get it.

Times today are difficult. Some of us may have adequate support from family, friends, or local agencies. And some of us may not. Dig deep. Look honestly at your challenges. What steps can you take to self-correct?

If you cannot pay the rent or mortgage and a local agency has not come through, what else can you do? Some industries are booming during this crisis. Grab your face mask and gloves and deliver groceries to those who need it. Walk the pets of owners who are too afraid to go out. Care for the children of moms and dads on the frontlines.

In many ways, we are dealing with much loss and stagnation. But through grit and determination, there are also opportunities to dig deep and survive. If you are not sure where to begin—grab your journal and brainstorm. First, vent your fears, worries, and frustrations. Get it all off your chest. Then, list possible solutions. Google it if you need to. Dream big. Start small.

NEXT STEPS: Journal and reflect – If you could go back to the 12-year-old version of yourself, what advice would you give?

Grit, the ability to persevere, will carry you through the darkest times.

God and Country

"Keep your head up. God gives his hardest battles to his strongest soldiers."— Author Unknown

To know the Divine is to know yourself. There is this part of us untouched by the world. There is no time or space in this center. There is no hate or yearning in this center. It just is.

Having a relationship with God does not require a specific location, pastor, or holy text. All you need is the desire and the will. If you were not formally trained in a particular faith, explore the options in your community or country to build your connection to the Source. With the internet, you may even consider a more global view and tradition you had not previously considered.

At times, it may feel as if the world spins in chaos and uncertainty, but God is always there. Let go of the need to predict the future or to have control over the actions of others. You have yourself and your spiritual connection. You have a connection that does not need to be explained or defended to family, friends, and co-workers. It is just for you. You may keep it as private or public as you choose.

If you can love and respect yourself, you can love and respect God. It is one and the same. Love has no limits or boundaries. No matter the state of the world around you, you are still here. You are in a safe place where you can take time to read this book. There is a purpose to your life. Accept it. Believe it.

Keep your head up!

NEXT STEPS: Say "thank you" for what is going well in your life, with no complaints.

To know the Divine is to know yourself.

The Power of Gratitude

Practicing gratitude is an extremely effective tool for coping during a crisis. Regularly expressing thankfulness also helps you ride the peaks and valleys in life. There are different ways to express feeling blessed. Gratitude journaling will deliver most if not all the benefits.

The dictionary definition of gratitude states: "the quality of being thankful; readiness to show appreciation for and to return kindness." Simply put, whether you are having a good day or bad day, you find a few things to appreciate in your life. You can be thankful that you woke up in good health when others may be struggling. You can be thankful for having food in the refrigerator when others do without. You can be grateful for having access to family through technology when others live in a drop zone.

Journaling every day is a great habit to start. Expressing gratitude through writing has a wealth of benefits. For example, you may experience the following:

1. Boost your long-term well-being, encouraging exercise, reducing physical pain and symptoms, and increasing both length and quality of sleep
2. Increase your optimism and, indirectly, your happiness and health
3. Make you friendlier, more open, and expand your social support network
4. Help you make progress toward your goals

Gratitude journaling requires little resources. There are free mobile apps where you can log your daily appreciation. Every day pick three things you are grateful for – no matter how large or small. Express what you are grateful for and the "because." Adding the why is important and sparks your "feel good" brain center.

NEXT STEPS: Write a thank you note to someone who did you favor, no matter how large or small.

Regularly expressing thankfulness also helps you ride the peaks and valleys in life.

Whether you are a father, uncle, or nephew, your time and attention towards the children in your family is priceless! You do not need to wait until summer vacation to start making a powerful difference. The benefits to spending time with children are endless, but a few reasons are listed here.

It builds children's self-esteem

Children who spend time with family in activities together build a positive sense of self-worth. When children feel that they are valued, they feel more positive about themselves. Family activities do not have to be expensive trips to be meaningful, the important part is just being together.

It strengthens family bonds

Families who share everyday activities together form strong, emotional ties. Studies have found that families who enjoy group activities together share a stronger emotional bond as well as an ability to adapt well to challenging situations as a family.

It develops positive behavior

Children and adolescents who spend more time with positive adults are less likely to get involved in risky behavior. According to studies done by the *National Center on Addiction and Substance Abuse via Arizona State University,* teens who have infrequent family dinners are twice as likely to use tobacco, nearly twice as likely to use alcohol and one and a half times more likely to use marijuana.

It encourages communication

When you spend time with the children in your family you are fostering an environment for open communication. Good communication is important for children to feel comfortable with talking to about anything. Simply asking a child how their day ask gone can make a big difference.

Children learn by example. If you are setting a good example for them by spending quality time together, they are more likely to adopt those behaviors in other relationships in their lives.

NEXT STEPS: Schedule a "play date" with a child or children in your family.

Whether you are a father, uncle, or nephew, your time and attention towards the children in your family is priceless!

The Pleasure of Pets

"If having a soul means being able to feel love and loyalty and gratitude, then animals are better off than a lot of humans."—James Herriot

Dogs rock! Cats rock! Horses are beautiful. Behold the stoicism of the iguana. No matter your animal preference, having a pet at home can bring endless love, companionship, and moments of good ole fashion humor.

The Benefits of Pet Ownership

Studies have shown that the bond between people and their pets can increase fitness, lower stress, and bring happiness to their owners. Some of the health benefits of having a pet include:

- Decreased blood pressure
- Decreased cholesterol levels
- Decreased feelings of loneliness
- Increased opportunities for exercise and outdoor activities
- Increased opportunities for socialization

Pick the Right Pet

Before adopting a new pet, make sure that it is the right one for you and your family. Do some research beforehand about the specific needs of the animal. Ask yourself these questions before getting a pet:

- How long will this animal live?
- What does the pet eat?
- How much exercise does the pet need?
- How large will it become?
- How much will it cost for veterinary care?
- Do I have enough time to properly care for and clean up after the pet?
- What type of habitat does this pet need to be healthy?
- What type of exercise does this pet need?
- Are pets allowed in my house, apartment, or condominium?

- Are there young children, older people, or people with weak immune systems who will care for or be around the pet?

Once you have your done due diligence, and checked all the important boxes, pick the animal that shows *enthusiasm* for joining your family.

Source: Centers for Disease Control and Prevention, Healthy People, Healthy Pets

NEXT STEPS: If you are unable to have a pet at home, consider volunteering at the local animal shelter and enjoy the free love.

No matter your animal preference, having a pet at home can bring endless love, companionship, and moments of good ole fashion humor.

Hidden Deep in the Man Cave

"To have passed through life and never experience solitude is to have never known oneself. To have never known oneself is to have never known anyone." – Joseph Krutch

No matter your marital status or relationship status, there are great benefits to having alone time. Here are just a few science-backed reasons for spending time alone:

1. Alone time increases empathy.

When you spend time with a certain circle of friends or your co-workers, you develop a "we vs. them" mentality. Spending time alone helps you develop more compassion for people who may not fit into your "inner circle."

2. Solitude increases productivity.

Although so many offices have started creating open floor plans so everyone can communicate more easily, studies show being surrounded by people kills productivity. People perform better when they have a little privacy.

3. Solitude sparks creativity.

There is a reason a lot of authors or artists want to go to a cabin in the woods or a private studio to work. Being alone with your thoughts gives your brain a chance to wander, which can help you become more creative.

4. Being alone can help you build mental strength.

We are social creatures, and it is important for us to have strong connections with other people. But solitude may be just as important. Studies show the ability to tolerate alone time has been linked to increased happiness, better life satisfaction, and improved stress management. People who enjoy alone time experience less depression.

6. Being alone gives you an opportunity to plan your life.

Spending time alone can give you a chance to ensure there is a purpose to all your hustling and bustling. Quiet space provides an opportunity think about your goals, your progress, and changes you want to make in your life.

7. Solitude helps you know yourself.

Being alone helps you become more comfortable in your own skin. When you are by yourself, you can make choices without outside influences. And that will help you develop more insight into who you are as a person.

Source: Forbes Magazine 2017

NEXT STEPS: Sit in your man cave with this book.

No matter your marital status or relationship status, there are great benefits to having alone time.

DATING AND RELATIONSHIPS

Love and Independence

She loves me. She loves me not. He loves me. He loves me not.

Love of self eliminates the need to be approved and accepted by others. You can just BE.

What is self-love? When you love yourself, you accept your strengths and weakness. You can always strive to be better, but perfection is an illusion. Sometimes all hell breaks loose, and things get messy. But that is part of life. You laugh it off. You cry and get tissue. You get mad and scream in your car. But then you bounce back and keep at it.

Having love of self, also means you understand that the world does not owe you anything. It is not another person's responsibility to make you happy or entertain you. Do not expect someone to make radical changes to accommodate you and your desires. You have the power obtain your own happiness.

How do you develop self-love? At some point, you take a hard look at who you are in life. What makes you strong? What makes you falter? Then balance the line between what is healthy and excessive. Setting boundaries around difficult people and difficult situations is important. Some challenges in life are necessary, but if a person or situation regularly upsets you, cut them out.

Create the opportunity for daily pleasures. You can love dark chocolate and have a bite after dinner. But you might not want to eat a whole bar, every day, indefinitely. Try the decadent hand cream that comes in the tiny jar. You might not use it every day, all day long, but maybe slather it on before bed. See the sunrise on a Sunday morning. However, it may not be something you can commit to every day with work, family, etc. Start small, carve out the time, enjoy daily pleasures.

NEXT STEPS: Enjoy the following articles about dating and relationships—unconditional love starts with you.

Love of self eliminates the need to be approved and accepted by others.

Building Trust, Part 1

"Trust takes years to build, seconds to break, and forever to repair."
– Author Unknown

Trust and communication are the key to any successful relationship. When you first start dating someone, you want to bring your A game. You want to appear attractive, successful, confident, and more. Never, never start a relationship with deception and expect to be forgiven later.

Here are a few tips and strategies to building trust in a relationship according to *Positive Psychology:*

Be true to your word and follow through with your actions

The point of building trust is for others to believe what you say. Keep in mind, however, that building trust requires not only keeping the promises you make but also not making promises you are unable to keep.

Learn how to communicate effectively with others

Poor communication is a major reason why relationships break down. Good communication includes being clear about what you have or have not committed to and what has been agreed upon. Building trust is not without risk. It involves allowing both you and others taking risks to prove trustworthiness.

Remind yourself that it takes time to build and earn trust

Building trust is a daily commitment. Do not make the mistake of expecting too much too soon. To build trust, first take small steps and take on small commitments and then, as trust grows, you will be more at ease with making and accepting bigger commitments. Put trust in, and you will generally get trust in return.

Take time to make decisions and think before acting too quickly

Only make commitments that you are happy to agree to. Have the courage to say "no," even when it disappoints someone. If you agree to something and cannot follow through, everyone involved is worse off.

Value the relationships that you have—and do not take them for granted

Trust often results from consistency. We tend to have the most trust in people who are there for us consistently through good times and bad. Regularly showing someone that you are there for them is an effective way to build trust.

NEXT STEPS: Be clear about your romantic intentions towards the person you are dating or in a relationship with. State them out loud. Transparency is good.

"Trust takes years to build, seconds to break, and forever to repair." – Author Unknown

Building Trust, Part 2

"Pain changes people, it makes them trust less, overthink more, and shut people out."

– Author Unknown

Unless you meet and marry your soul mate during high school, chances are you have had failed relationship and been hurt. Some people bounce back more easily from disappointing relationships than others. If you are dating a good but overly cautious person, give it time. Do not take the walls personal. Do not expect the person to tell you their whole life story in the first or second date. More than likely, you are dealing with someone who has been deeply hurt in love, is willing to try again, but needs time. Be patient.

Here are more tips and strategies to building trust in a relationship:

Always be honest

The message you convey should always, always be the truth. If you are caught telling a lie, no matter how small, your trustworthiness will be diminished.

Help people whenever you can

Helping another person, even if it provides no benefit to you, builds trust. Authentic kindness helps to build trust.

Do not hide your feelings

Being open about your emotions is often an effective way to build trust. Furthermore, if people know that you care, they are more likely to trust you. Emotional intelligence plays a role in building trust. Acknowledging your feelings, learning the lessons that prevail, and taking productive action means that you will not deny reality—this is the key to building trust.

Always do what you believe to be right

Doing something purely for approval means sacrificing your own values and beliefs. This decreases trust in yourself, your values, and your beliefs. Always doing what you believe is right, even when others disagree, will lead others to respect your honesty. Interestingly, when building trust, you must be willing to upset others on occasion. People tend not to trust those who simply say whatever they think others want to hear.

Admit your mistakes

When you attempt to hide your mistakes, people know that you are being dishonest. By being open, you show your vulnerable side, and this helps build trust with other people. This is because they perceive you to be more like them—everyone makes mistakes. When all that a person sees is the "perfection" you project, they likely will not trust you.

NEXT STEPS: Be patient with your crush and no matter what, do no harm.

"Pain changes people, it makes them trust less, overthink more, and shut people out."

– Author Unknown

Emotional IQ and Relationships

Emotional IQ is needed to have successful relationships with family, friends, and lovers. Emotional intelligence is the ability to understand, use, and manage your own emotions in positive ways to relieve stress, communicate effectively, empathize with others, overcome challenges, and defuse conflict.

Emotional IQ helps you build stronger relationships, succeed at school, and work, and achieve your career and personal goals. It can also help you to connect with your feelings, turn intention into action, and make informed decisions about what matters most to you.

So how can you build your emotional IQ that leads to great love IQ? Here are suggestions according to online relationships experts, *Help Guide.*

Observe how you react to people. Do you rush to judgment before you know all the facts? Do you stereotype? Look honestly at how you think and interact with other people. Try to put yourself in their place and be more open and accepting of their perspectives and needs.

Do a self-evaluation. Try out our emotional intelligence quiz. What are your weaknesses? Are you willing to accept that you are not perfect and that you could work on some areas to make yourself a better person? Have the courage to look at yourself honestly – it can change your life.

Examine how you react to stressful situations. Do you become upset every time there is a delay or something does not happen the way you want? Do you blame others or become angry at them, even when it is not their fault? The ability to stay calm and in control in difficult situations is highly valued – in the business world and outside it. Keep your emotions under control when things go wrong.

Take responsibility for your actions. If you hurt someone's feelings, apologize directly – do not ignore what you did or avoid the person. People are usually more willing to forgive and forget if you make an honest attempt to make things right.

Examine how your actions will affect others – before you take those actions. If your decision will impact others, put yourself in their place. How will they feel if you do this? Would you want that experience? If you must take the action, how can you help others deal with the effects?

The good news is that emotional intelligence can be learned and developed!

NEXT STEPS: Read the next article to see how you can build your emotional IQ and be more successful in love.

Emotional IQ is needed to have successful relationships with family, friends, and lovers.

Grow Your Emotional IQ and Grow Your Love IQ

"Relationships don't last because of the good times; they last because the hard times were handled with love and care." – Author Unknown

Love relationships are not without certain challenges and obstacles. How you handle the difficult times determines the longevity of your relationship. Nobody is perfect. Your partner needs to know that even when he or she makes a mistake, you will still have love and trust.

To grow your emotional IQ and in turn have more love in your life, try the following tips and strategies:

Observe how you react to people. Do you rush to judgment before you know all the facts? Do you stereotype? Look honestly at how you think and interact with other people. Try to put yourself in their place and be more open and accepting of their perspectives and needs.

Look at your work environment. Do you seek attention for your accomplishments? Humility can be a wonderful quality, and it does not mean that you are shy or lack self-confidence. When you practice humility, you say that you know what you did, and you can be quietly confident about it. Give others a chance to shine – put the focus on them, and do not worry too much about getting praise for yourself.

Do a self-evaluation. Try out our emotional intelligence quiz. What are your weaknesses? Are you willing to accept that you are not perfect and that you could work on some areas to make yourself a better person? Have the courage to look at yourself honestly – it can change your life.

Examine how you react to stressful situations. Do you become upset every time there is a delay or something does not happen the way you want? Do you blame others or become angry at them, even when it is not their fault? The ability to stay calm and in control in difficult situations is highly valued – in the business world and outside it. Keep your emotions under control when things go wrong.

Take responsibility for your actions. If you hurt someone's feelings, apologize directly – do not ignore what you did or avoid the person.

People are usually more willing to forgive and forget if you make an honest attempt to make things right.

Examine how your actions will affect others – before you take those actions. If your decision will impact others, put yourself in their place. How will they feel if you do this? Would you want that experience? If you must take the action, how can you help others deal with the effects?

NEXT STEPS: What can you do today, to be a more loving and understanding friend or partner?

How you handle the difficult times determines the longevity of your relationship.

Love Letters During COVID-19

"To write a good love letter, you ought to begin without knowing what you mean to say, and to finish without knowing what you have written." –Jean-Jacques Rousseau

It is believed that the act of writing can evoke feelings of love in the writer. A love letter has no formal rules around form, length, or style. You can write a love letter that is long, passionate, poetic—a real labor of love. You can write a love letter that is short with a few powerful words in a text. It is up to the writer to decide on the type of message to be communicated.

What is love? You can write about devotion, ambition, obsession, disappointment, forgiveness, etc. Love is many things to many people.

For You

We are living during uncertain times. Write a love letter to yourself of motivation, encouragement, and selfcare. Revel in the splendor of knowing who you are, what you stand for, and living your life as you see fit. Describe the freedom of being able to stand strong and imperfect during difficult times.

For Your Partner

You may be at a distance from your partner. Or you may be too close in quarantine with your partner. Write a love letter of forgiveness, commitment, and fantasy. Remember better times and make plans for an exciting future. Write a romantic scene for a world without corona and share it with your loved one.

For Your Family and Friends

All love does not have to be romantic. We can love our family. We can love our friends. Love is listening with our ears and our hearts. Love is making the effort to understand the other person. Write love and support notes to friends who may be unemployed or furloughed. Write loving words to family who may sick and in recovery. Create a word collage of love for children going back to school who may be nervous about a different kind of school year.

As the world spins, we need more love and kindness.

NEXT STEPS: Find real stationary and write a love letter to yourself, your partner, or a family member.

It is believed that the act of writing can evoke feelings of love in the writer.

Taming the Hen Party – Part 1

Congratulations! The term "hen party" is officially in the dictionary. What does it mean?

hen party (noun) Definition of hen party: a party for women only

No matter your sexual orientation, if you are dating a woman, beware the hen party. Until you say, "I love you," the messy details of who you are as a boyfriend are discussed among the girls solely for their entertainment. So, how do you tame the hen party and avoid character assassination?

Rule #1: Never diss the friend of your partner

Your partner might have the most annoying girlfriend from the Black Lagoon. Never speak on it! She had that friend before you. They have a history. Avoid giving the impression that you cannot get along with a long-standing friendship. Your girlfriend will secretly wonder if she will have to choose between you and the best friend down the road.

Rule #2: Never make negative generalizations about women

No matter your experiences with women as friends, lovers, and family—never make broad negative generalizations about women. The hen party will crucify you for this. One wrong statement about women of the world can send them into a man bashing spiral that will last for hours, days, maybe more. When your woman returns to you from the hen party, there is going to be an invisible wall, that can only be broken down with good d*ck skills.

Rule #3: Do not give a cheap gift in the first year of your relationship

Hopefully, you are employed while you are dating. Money does not make the man, but do not give a cheap gift during the first year of your relationship with a woman. The hen party will assume that the value of the gift represents the value you place on your girlfriend and the relationship. If you cannot afford diamonds, champagne, and lace, then plan gifts that make wonderful memories. If you have any musical talent, consider singing a song, playing an instrument, and shedding a sentimental man tear. If you can do more than boil water, consider going to the grocery store, and cooking at 3- course meal, that includes a nice dessert. Set the table with real plates, cloth napkins, and inexpensive candles. If social media is your thing, consider collecting and printing all the pictures of you and your love, make a giant collage, and present it during the appropriate holiday.

NEXT STEPS: Retrace your steps. Have you said anything negative about the members of the hen party? If you have, correct it immediately.

No matter your sexual orientation, if you are dating a woman, beware the hen party.

Taming the Hen Party – Part 2

So now that you know the major pitfalls of the hen party, what can you do to make sure they sing your praises?

Rule #4: Compliment small positive changes

Everyone gets a "congratulations" for big changes like a new job, new apartment, or new haircut. Complimenting the obvious is easy. The hen party will fall out of their seats if you notice and compliment small changes by your partner. For example, if your lover cooks you a spaghetti dinner and replaces the dried parmesan with freshly grated parmesan Reggiano cheese, give a compliment. If your girlfriend mostly wears neutral colors and black, then one day she is sporting a deep red blouse, give a compliment. Your girlfriend and the hen party will love you and sing your praises when you notice the small stuff. Remember to only compliment, what you want *more* of.

Rule #5: Give hugs and kisses for bad days

Eh, we all have our bad days. That great promotion at work goes to a co-worker. The washing machine breaks down and floods the basement. The dog chews a favorite pair of pumps. Give hugs and kisses for bad days. You might not always have a great motivational speech. You might not be able to fix it. Just give some hugs and kisses.

Rule #6: Perform random acts of service

There is a lot of publicity these days that women want to feel empowered, fearless, and competent. It is true. But can you kill that spider over there? Open this pickle jar? Do some dishes? Thank you, very much.

NEXT STEPS: Check in with yourself. When was the last time the hen party smiled at you? What can you do today to get one smile?

The hen party will fall out of their seats if you notice and compliment small changes by your partner.

Saucy Girlfriends

"Jessica Rabbit: You don't know how hard it is being a woman looking the way I do." –Who Framed Roger Rabbit, 1988

In the 1988 film, *Who Framed Roger Rabbit*, Jessica Rabbit is this red-headed, voluptuous vixen, that makes the men drool and lose all reason. Whatever your sexual orientation if you are dating a woman, beware of the saucy, sexy girlfriend. This is the attractive friend who smiles at you, chats with you, spends time with you and your partner—and indirectly strokes your ego. This article is following the *"Taming the Hen Party"* segment for a reason.

If you are being a good boyfriend, husband, lover, whatever your title, your partner is sharing good stories with her friends. True friends congratulate the relationship success. Another kind of friend might slide up next to you wanting to get a sample of the goods. Beware! Do not fall for this unless you want your primary relationship to end.

If you have ever been single for a period, you know how it seems to hang over you in different ways. When you go on dates, the other person always wants to know *why* you are single in the first place. Or the other person wants to know how *long* you have been single. If you do not give a good reason for being single, you indirectly have a *bad reference* from the last relationship. If you have been single too long, then that can also be perceived as a *red flag* that you might not be relationship material. Now, when you are in a relationship and getting good publicity—*yum, yum gimme some.* You have a stamp of approval. It is like needing have a good credit score to get more credit cards.

So, when you are in a good relationship, you will stand out to saucy girlfriends and other single women who do not mind a little backstabbing to catch a man. Once again, do not fall for this, unless you want your primary relationship to end. This type of behavior only leads to a lifestyle of quantity over quality. Plus, karma is a real b*tch! If you work through the process of carefully choosing the right partner, stick with the relationship through the normal ups and downs of life. If you decide to end the relationship, do the honorable thing, and make a clean break before jumping into a new connection.

NEXT STEPS: Never spend a lot of time alone with a saucy girlfriend.

If you are being a good boyfriend, husband, lover, whatever your title, your partner is sharing good stories with her friends.

Celebrity Fantasies

There is perception and there is truth. We often write grand "stories" about ourselves and the people around us—to be retold repeatedly in our minds. We often develop fantasies when dealing with other people. In these illusions, we are quick to make ourselves the hero.

When it comes to dating and relationships, half of us have no real-world role models. All we know about romantic love is what we see from celebrities, movies, magazines, and other forms of entertainment. Pop culture makes love and romance seem super easy. All you must do it is be cute, say the right thing during the first meeting, and *BLAM*, you are off having porn-star sex. Or you make the effort to have a relationship, give each other titles, and then somebody has a bad day. Your partner hurts your feelings for the first time, and man, the sky is falling. You cannot deal. You take off. It is time to find *new* love.

Please, please understand the difference between a celebrity fantasy and a true-blue romantic relationship. Despite, what you see in pop culture, a real relationship has peaks and valleys. There are misunderstandings, miscommunication, and a need for forgiveness from time to time. Your partner may have days where she is really rocking it and hot stuff on the runway. Then the next day she is having razor sharp stubble on her legs and slips fart when she thinks you are sleeping.

Nobody is perfect. You are not perfect. Your partner is not perfect. When you decide to enter a committed relationship with someone, the main goal is to build positive experiences and memories. Eventually, someone will have an illness, job difficulties, death in the family, or a pandemic will hit, and it will seem as if the world has gone to hell. But when it is true love, and you are in it for the right reasons. You ride the peaks and valleys and hold on. The good memories will carry you through until the storm clouds part and the sun shines again.

NEXT STEPS: Enjoy watching ABC's the Bachelor, but realize, you will most likely, *never* live that life. And it is okay.

When you decide to enter a committed relationship with someone, the main goal is to build positive experiences and memories.

Love in the Valley

Life by definition involves changes. Nothing last forever. Impermanence is a fact. Sometimes your partner has a temporary illness, job loss, or major change in their family. When you find your partner is struggling with the weight of the world, you must be the bigger person and love her or him in the valley.

The real danger of being in the valley is believing there is no way out. There is a way out, it just might take time. The myth of being in the valley is thinking you are alone. Everybody finds themselves in the valley from time to time, they just might not tell you about it. The illusion of being in the valley is that it only happens one time. Help your partner accept that it is part of life, embrace the highs, and remember the lessons to cope next time life is temporarily overwhelming.

What is love in the valley? Be a support to your partner. Know when to ask for help as it is needed, whether it is family or a paid professional. Maintain healthy boundaries. Do not allow yourself or the family to fall into crisis and you act as an emotional support. If the family is not up to that community event, do not go. Create positive routines around sleep, diet, and exercise. Everything is harder when you are tired, hungry, or achy. Venting difficult emotions is also love in the valley. Encourage your partner to journal, sing, garden, cook, make art – decide whatever it is that makes you both feel lighter.

NEXT STEPS: Check in with yourself. Are you okay? Check in with your partner. Is she/he okay?

Venting difficult emotions is also love in the valley.

Online Dating During COVID-19

Online dating sites have become super popular during COVID-19. It is safer than mingling face-to-face. It is easier to screen people before approaching them. You *think* you have more options.

Know your intentions for online and be honest with the other person before meeting. If you are looking for marriage, state that. If you are looking for a girlfriend, state that. If you just want to be friends with benefits, you also need to state that.

Frankly, a lot of online dating is men and women selling fantasies. Everybody wants to be loved. Everybody wants to be chosen. Beautiful pictures can be generated. It is harder to confirm who you are talking to until you meet face-to-face and spend real time together.

If you choose to date online seriously be reasonable. Guard your privacy. Do not advertise your home address, job location, or family members. If a person does not talk to you using their voice or get on webcam, it can be anybody. A she can be a he. A Virginia person can really be someone in the Himalayans. Watch out for money scams. A potential partner that is too good to be true, typically is. The other person can be selling you a fantasy and when you meet, they ask for a dollar figure.

It is this author's opinion that a lot of men who date online, do so because they do not have the courage to ask out their dream girl next door. If you have love or yearning for a person in your environment, skip the wild, wild west of online dating. Invest in the person you already like and respect.

NEXT STEPS: Are you paying a membership fee when the one you really want is next door?

Know your intentions for online and be honest with the other person before meeting.

God and Sex

You can love God. You can love sex. If you are monogamous and respectful, you will not go to hell. If you have any other intentions, this author cannot comment.

NEXT STEPS: God loves us as our imperfect selves. Our sins have already been paid for.

If you are monogamous and respectful, you will not go to hell.

White Lies

Unconditional love starts from within and it is a daily practice. We receive a lot of messages from pop culture about beauty, money, and how to be powerful in the world. Some of it is good stuff. A lot of it is bad and superficial. Depending on your circle of family and friends, it can be difficult to navigate.

If you haver partner, be a positive influence in that person's life. Help build a relationship of mutual respect, support, and unconditional love. If your partner ask you questions around beauty, talents, or future planning—motivate and encourage. Even if there is no perfectly detailed plan, project good intentions. Tell those little white lies.

NEXT STEPS: Give some hugs and kisses today.

Unconditional love starts from within and it is a daily practice.

Coffee Dates – Just Ask!

If you like someone, ask her out for a cup of coffee. Period.

Confidence is sexy. Yes, it is smart to chat and put out the nonverbal communication to see if someone is interested in you. But after a while, use your words, and ask for the coffee date. Many a great love has been lost and fizzled out due to lack of confidence. Women today do different things to feel empowered, strong, and smart. However, after a certain point, we do not want to be our own knight in shining armor.

If she says no, try someone else. If she says yes, you are rocking it!

NEXT STEPS: Wise up and step up!

If you like someone, ask her out for a cup of coffee. Period.

BUSINESS, CAREER, AND COMMUNITY

A Job Well Done

If you have the opportunity to be well-paid for your talents and abilities, that is awesome! If not, rock the job opportunity anyway! Fake it until you make it. Never settle for mediocrity in the workplace. Somebody is always watching even when you think your role is not that important.

How do you develop effective habits that will land you that dream job in the future?

Step 1: Pack your schedule.

Most people waste a LOT of time, usually 60 - 100 hours every week, because they have too much down time and are not busy enough.

Make a schedule. Schedule every 30 minutes and fill it to the brim with stuff; this can be stuff that makes you excited, it can be work, it can be sleep, it can be watching a movie, it can be learning to play an instrument, etc. Just pack it full so that you are the one in control of your time and so that you learn what you are capable of.

Step 2: Do things no one else is willing to do.

When someone says it cannot be done, or that it is impossible, you should be the first one in line to test it out. Test it, see if it is impossible, and then make it work out somehow. Become the person everyone goes to if they want something handled that is too hard.

Step 3: Learn more than anyone else.

Not just by studying in school, but especially about yourself, how to improve yourself, and how to master all the areas of your life. Study every single day. Learn at least for an hour a day by watching videos or reading, and you will be way more knowledgeable than the average person, which gives you more control over your life.

Step 4: Wake up earlier than everyone else.

If you can wake up early, it shows that you are in control of your life. Most mistakes, regrets, and bad decisions are made after 10 PM. Go to bed early so you can wake up early and make better decisions, which lead to a better life, which gets you out of "average."

Step 5: Never surrender on the things you truly want.

Most average people give up as soon as things get tough and then they complain that they never got what they wanted. Of course, things will get hard! You will cry, be frustrated, afraid, angry, and totally beaten to a pulp, but when the average person stops getting up, you must rise once more.

Step 6: Keep your plans *PRIVATE!*

Keep your hopes, dreams, and plans private! Do not broadcast to the world what you are trying to accomplish. Everyone who has settled into mediocrity will find ways to sabotage your efforts to your face and behind your back. Sad, but true. Keep your cards close. Put on your best poker face. Unless a particular person oversees the thing or opportunity you need at the time, it is simply nobody's business what you are up.

NEXT STEPS: Grab a piece of paper or open a writing app on your phone, what are your career goals for the next 90 days, six months, calendar year?

Keep your hopes, dreams, and plans private!

The Measure of a Man

integrity

1. *the quality of being honest and having strong moral principles; moral uprightness.*

The measure of a man is integrity. Having ethics in the workplace is crucial. Without integrity, you cannot be in a leadership position. Others will not follow you. Or the ones that follow you are as dishonest as you. Whether you are managing millions or volunteer donations—tell the truth!

Hopefully, the company you work for has a code of ethics and/or code of conduct in their employee handbook. Make sure you follow it. Do not require someone to coach you or train on the values. As a new hire, get a copy, read it, know it. As it is periodically updated, read it again.

The biggest lies people tell around business is money, sex, and power over others. In regards, to money, count the money right. Have a system of checks and balances so if any money turns up missing, you have proof it was not you! When it comes to sex in the workplace, you need to watch out for issues of sexual harassment. Love is blind, but it is better not to sh*t where you eat. Finally, every organization has office politics and office gossip. Do what you can to keep your personal business out of office gossip. Make sure you avoid office politics that subjugates you or others.

Also, even if you find yourself in an unsavory situation and you have the connections to stay out of trouble, karma is not your friend. One day, down the road, you will find yourself paying the price for how you were unfair to others. Do not join in, in making the workplace difficult. We all need the opportunity to provide food, shelter, and clothing for ourselves and our families.

NEXT STEPS: Get a copy of your company's employee handbook and read it again or maybe for the first time.

Whether you are managing millions or volunteer donations—tell the truth!

Team Cooperation vs Herd Mentality

Most employers today will tell you that they want employees that are team players. If you have been in the workforce for any length of time, you know it is important to go along to get along. *We all gotta eat.* However, there is a difference between being a team player and having a herd mentality in unethical situations.

What is herd mentality?

The Webster definition of herd mentality is "the tendency of the people in a group to think and behave in ways that conform with others in the group rather than as individuals." In simpler terms, you do what everybody else does even when it is simply, *stoopid.* If you work in a restaurant and your team lead says spit in the bad customer's drink, you do it to fit in, even though it is the wrong thing to do. If you are on a committee at work and the team lead is threatened and intimidated by the new hire, you withhold important company updates from the new hire, so they struggle to succeed. If you are working on a management project and the team lead has personal issues and is missing meetings, you slow down production, miss deadlines, to fit in with the weakest link and be liked.

Herd mentality skews towards the negative. Difficult personalities in the workplace have some charisma and the ability to lead others into misfortune. Watch out for this! If you find that your morality is constantly challenged in work situations, it might not be a good fit for you. Typically, you know if a job is a good fit in the first 90 days. Keep your eyes open for company snake charmers.

What is being a team player?

Being a team player is understanding the company's vision and goals to make positive strives to support the bigger picture. When the company wins, you win! Here are some strategies to be the right team player:

- Understand your role
- Embrace positive collaboration
- Hold yourself accountable

- Commit to the team
- Be flexible
- Be optimistic
- Back up goals with action

If you are working for a company that is the right fit, you embrace the challenge of supporting great people with healthy goals and values.

NEXT STEPS: Assess how you feel after a day of team cooperation. Do you feel motivated by good deeds or a little guilty by something you do not want your friends to know?

Being a team player is understanding the company’s vision and goals to make positive strives supporting the bigger picture.

Role Model—Be One!

In the world, we are slowly recovering from a pandemic. In the USA, we are exploring reform to stop racial injustice. Everybody has an opinion on how to bring about change. March here. Donate there. Tweet that.

Be a ROLE MODEL. If you care about your community and want to stop the spread of COVID-19, wear a mask every time. If you believe in racial equality, do not flinch when a person of color does not smile through an offense. Sit down. Listen. Hear what he/she has to say.

Do what you can as you can. It does not really require you to spend to spend money if you do not have the finances. It does not require you to step out in the streets if you have children or vulnerable family at home. Do not minimize the need for revolution down to a social media tweet or post.

Start SMALL. Get really clear about what you believe. Explore your faith, values, and desires for the kind of nation you want to live in. Write it down! Use a journal to address every issue in your community that bothers you.

Next, outline a vision of that hero beating the challenges. What would this person do every day, every week, and every month? Do not edit yourself. Get it all down on paper. Now you need to realize, YOU are that hero. You are the person that can take a stand in large and small ways.

If you see an injustice, speak on it, write about it, go to the other person, and ask, "Are you okay?" If you see someone bullied in the workplace, do not join in, do not turn a blind eye. Behind the scenes, maybe you help that person proofread an important memo. Maybe you invite your neighbor over for dinner, who has just lost his job.

The options are endless. It is up to you. This is how we ALL take a stand.

NEXT STEPS: What is one small thing you can do today to make your community better?

Be a role model. Start small.

True Leadership

Leadership has nothing to do with seniority or one's position in the hierarchy of a company. Leadership does not automatically happen when you reach a certain pay grade. Hopefully, you find it there, but there are no guarantees. Leadership has nothing to do with titles.

A leader has followers. Often, the teams follow by example.

Leaders have vision. Every spring you have a vision for a garden, and with lots of work carrots and tomatoes become a reality.

Leaders empower others. You want a team of competent independent adults. Give them the tools to make smart decisions, as needed, without being timid or hesitating.

Leadership is influence. You walk the walk and talk the talk. Leaders model the positive behavior they want to see from others. Leaders coach and motivate others to greatness without self-comparison.

There are many different leadership skills required in the workplace, but the most in-demand ones include:

- Active listening
- Empathy
- The ability to share clear messages and make complex ideas easy to understand for everyone
- Strategic thinking skills
- Creativity
- The ability to inspire and convince others
- Flexibility

There is the controversy that some leaders are born while others are made. It is all a matter of perception and motivation. If you believe you are a leader, you are a leader. Use the tools and resources in your workplace or community to be an awesome one. It takes practice and commitment to a greater good.

NEXT STEPS: How can you be a better leader in the workplace, community, family, or place of worship?

Leadership is influence. You walk the walk and talk the talk.

Community Service

It is important to have men involved in their communities. Traditionally men are seen as providers and focus on paid opportunities, but there are great benefits to performing community service. A few benefits include:

- Community Service Helps Connect to the Community
- It Benefits Your Career Prospects
- Community Service Raises Social Awareness
- Community Service Establishes Contacts and Friendships
- Community Service Helps Improve Your Skills

There are different options for performing community service whether you have the time weekly, monthly, or in certain seasons:

- Volunteer at your local library
- Volunteer to chaperone a field trip
- Volunteer with a local nonprofit
- Volunteer at an animal shelter
- Volunteer at a community center
- Volunteer as a lifeguard
- Volunteer to be a crossing guard
- Volunteer to do social media for a local organization

And sometimes, just sometimes, you have *fun* completing community service projects. It is a great way to meet new people if you are new to an area or trying to break out of a rut. If you are single, there are tons of single people volunteering in their free time.

NEXT STEPS: Consider your schedule and personal interests. How would you like to get involved today?

And sometimes, just sometimes, you have *fun* completing community service projects.

The Next Generation and You! Part 1

The youth are our future. No matter your age, there is always a generation behind you coming up. Remember what may seem ordinary or commonplace to you, is new to the next generation. There are tons of books, magazines, and resources describing the characteristics of each new generation.

The purpose of this article is not to stereotype young people or pigeon-hole them. However, but there are eight traits needed in modern leaders:

#1: Have a clear vision

Not all managers are leaders, and not all leaders are managers. The main difference between the two categories is that managers have objectives, while leaders have a vision. Leaders should have a clear understanding of themselves, know their strengthens and weaknesses and spend an important part of their efforts in learning and continue building their capacity. By focusing on setting a vision and showing a desire to improve, grow and inspire, leaders look at the future beyond the short goals and obstacles, thus helping them to persevere and bring everyone along.

#2: Develop your team

More than 70% of a leader's time should be spent in managing people and finding ways to develop them. The primary role of a leader is to make sure that their team members have the resources and the capacity to do their jobs while thinking on how to create synergies between the team members. It is important also to note that personal and professional development is crucial in developing a strong team, thus should be a priority in leading a healthy team.

#3: Mentor your successor

It is often believed that if managers are doing a good job, then they should stay in the same position forever. Managers often thus maintain the status quo, which is not acceptable in today's world. Leaders doing a good job are the ones who are training their colleagues to take over. In any organization, life positions should be abolished moving forward. Leaders should be challenged in new positions, or at least get more responsibility, and, thus, be pushed outside of their comfort zones vertically and horizontally.

#4: Create a safe space

It is important to build a safe space for the whole team, a space where everyone is valued and where they can feel true to themselves. It is the duty of leaders to create a safe space where their colleagues are not afraid to share their disagreement and can challenge the leaders. Part of creating the safe space is attributing success to the team and taking responsibility and blame for failure. If there is a failure, it is the leaders' fault. If there is a success, it is thanks to the team's hard work.

NEXT STEPS: Do a little research on emotional IQ to better respond to different personalities in the workplace.

It is important to build a safe space for the whole team, a space where everyone is valued and where they can feel true to themselves.

The Next Generation and You! Part 1

Supporting the next generation takes heart and drive. Remember to have fun, light conversation with youth in the workplace, community, and extended family. Stay on topic of issues that are important to young people. Here, we continue with important leadership qualities needed to lead everyone, including the next generation:

#1: Do not micromanage

What happens when leaders are away? The power of a successful team can be known when the leaders are not in the office. Is the manager contacted for every single decision? Are the teams taking full charge of their responsibility? Do they have the guts to take decisions? Will leaders back their team's decisions once back? A successful team should have the capacity to function even when their leader is not around and should be able to take decisions within their sphere and job description.

#2: Give productive feedback

Leaders should always share honest feedback with their colleagues. Effective communication is a crucial trait of a leader. Different feedback has different effect on people. Adapting the language and the words to every colleague is important to communicate the vision within the capability and task of every single person. Detailed or general and focusing on one group of people might leave others behind. In the same line, there should open channels of productive feedback between all members of the team. Leaders should also crave feedback, as it is their tool to develop themselves.

#3: Be a follower

The best leaders are the best followers. When entrusting anyone with a responsibility, a leader is also a person who knows how to step down and follow others' leadership. In a whole, we should look at leadership as a process where a team works towards an inspiring vision, beyond individuals.

NEXT STEPS: The next time you are asked for honest feedback in the workplace, give two positives, and one area of improvement.

Remember to have fun, light conversation with youth in the workplace, community, and extended family.

Day by Day Strength

"With the new day comes new strength and new thoughts." -Eleanor Roosevelt

What is happening next week? Next month? Next year? Sometimes, we worry and obsess so much about the future, we forget today is here. Today is…HERE. Day by day strength means being grounded in the present and planting seeds for the future.

The best of us might have long-range plans, vision boards, to do list, and a marked-up calendar. But, nothing happens without small steady steps towards progress. Whether your goal is to be a fitter you, Rockstar employee, or more organized parent – take it day by day.

We are summation of our daily habits. There is no guarantee of a tomorrow, next month, or next season. We have no immediate control over the weather, pandemics, international economies as ordinary citizens. Work with what you have. Write down daily goals. Leave room for missteps and those moments where we just "don't feel like it."

At times we feel like we must carry the weight of the world on our shoulders. But you just need to carry yourself through this moment. What is necessary in this moment? Do you have what you need to happy and whole in this moment? Are the people you love safe and well fed?

Whenever you come upon this post, stop for a moment, take a deep breath, and look around. Today is…HERE. What can you accomplish in this moment, without too much fuss?

NEXT STEPS: Sit for a minute and just breathe.

We are summation of our daily habits.

The Power of Words

Words have power. You can build bridges or destroy with the power of words. Before you speak to others, ask yourself—Is it true? Is it kind? Is it inspiring? Is it necessary? Be a role model of integrity, charisma, and good emotional IQ. Overtime, you will draw in like minds and hopefully build a community where people motivate and encourage others to be their best.

Avoid pitfalls

In the workplace, communities, and families, we have plenty of *Debbie Downers.* Criticizing and complaining is easy. Office gossip is often co-workers using their free time to claim victimhood and complain and complain about the people around them. Scientific studies show that human beings skew negative. We take small disappointments and make them super large to avoid the danger in the future. Do not join in spirals of spoken negativity!

How to give positive feedback

If given the opportunity to give feedback, take the time to consider the project or situation being discussed. Share two positives and one area of concern. People are easily overwhelmed and discouraged from the critique of others. A person has the focus and energy to address one to two areas of improvement. If you are in a management position, you want to motivate your team to do better and not demoralize them into mediocrity.

How to connect emotionally with others

Depending on the circumstances, when you meet new people you must consider the environment and the temperament of this stranger. It is much better to discuss universal topics that anyone can speak on. Some examples include the weather, good food at an event, inspiring presentations, and even music hits. Do not require a stranger to share their sensitive personal characteristics like marital status, child status, age, etc. for your entertainment. If there is something personal you with to know in good faith, try telling a story about yourself first. If the other person feels comfortable, he or she will share. If they do not, it is nothing personal. Finally, give it time. You never know what someone else is going through. And sometimes people are simply preoccupied with different issues in their world. Not to stereotype, but some private people take a little more time to warm up and connect. Private people, sometimes labeled introverts, often have the most genuine, soft hearts and they protect it.

NEXT STEPS: Give a compliment to a total stranger with no strings attached.

You can build bridges or destroy with the power of words.

He Ain't Heavy, He's My Brother

The road is long
With many a winding turn
That leads us to who knows where
Who knows where
But I'm strong
Strong enough to carry him
He ain't heavy, he's my brother

Song Lyrics by Bob Russell / Bobby Scott

Cooperation is the key to surviving in families, communities, and the workplace. Having empathy for others means you accept differences in appearance, communication style, and thoughts and opinions. Everybody has a personal story based on a past, present, and future. Whether this story is shared with you or not, know it is there.

"He ain't heavy, he's my brother," is about supporting the people around you in healthy, positive ways. If you and your personal needs are met, reach back, and help someone else. How deep you dig to help someone else, depends on you and your circumstances. Some people volunteer at a local food bank once the month. Some people donate free change to charity organizations. Some people talk on their cell phone at midnight with a friend in need. There is no right or wrong way to reach back and help others, it all depends on what you can give.

The best strategy to supporting others, is to do it with no strings attached. How you choose to help is your business. Do not expect or ask for anything in return. Also be careful about being a martyr. Do not carry another person "on your back" until you are worn out and dragging yourself through life. You also must understand that at some point a person must learn how to stand strong in this world and be self-sufficient.

NEXT STEPS: How are you feeling? If your personal needs are met, find a way to help your neighbor.

Cooperation is the key to surviving in families, communities, and the workplace.

The End

Thank you for reading!

www.ingramcontent.com/pod-product-compliance
Lightning Source LLC
LaVergne TN
LVHW010624100826
845148LV00014B/3098

9781733483698